jugular

words of warfare

Rebecca Anne Perry

Jugular – words of warfare

© Copyright 2019 by Rebecca Anne Perry

All rights reserved. No part of this publication may be reproduced, stored in a retrieval system or transmitted in any form or by any means – for example electronic, photocopy, recording – without prior written permission of the author. The only exception is brief quotations in printed reviews.

Perry 2 Publishing
2711 N Sepulveda Blvd. #726
Manhattan Beach, CA 90266

ISBN: 978-0-578-58327-3

All Scripture quotations, unless otherwise indicated, are taken from the Holy Bible, New International Version®, NIV®. Copyright ©1973, 1978, 1984, 2011 by Biblica, Inc.™ Used by permission of Zondervan. All rights reserved worldwide. www.zondervan.com The "NIV" and "New International Version" are trademarks registered in the United States Patent and Trademark Office by Biblica, Inc.™

Scripture quotations marked (NLT) are taken from the Holy Bible, New Living Translation, copyright ©1996, 2004, 2015 by Tyndale House Foundation. Used by permission of Tyndale House Publishers, Inc., Carol Stream, Illinois 60188. All rights reserved.

For more information about Rebecca, please visit:

RebeccaAnnePerry.com

Dedications

To all the prayer warriors

To all the supernatural battle-tested brave ones

To all the those who stand in the gap

To all those who know the victory is already theirs

To all those who dance on the crashing waves

To all those who make their home in the storm

To all those who are not of this world

For God so loved the world that he gave his one and only Son, that whoever believes in him shall not perish but have eternal life.
~ John 3:16

Introduction

This is a book of poetry about and in response to spiritual warfare that I've experience in my life and witnessed in the lives of those around me. This book is about fighting *from* victory, not *for* victory, because the Lord has already won the victory for us at the cross and in His resurrection. This book is about pursuing the Father's heart in the midst of battle and finding refuge in His eyes in the midst of the storm.

My intention in writing this book, in imparting these warrior poems and sharing my story is to inspire others to fiercely fight the enemy (the devil) and stand in the gap (pray) for humanity. Also, I pray that this book provokes in unbelievers a holy jealousy for and deep longing to know the Lord.

This book began, as my previous book did, with these poems simply flowing from and pouring out of my heart as I wrestled with the Lord on my personal faith journey. Sometimes it's as if poetry is the only expression that makes sense to me, because it's all that comes out of me. The deeper the pain and questioning, the more powerful and passionate is the poetry.

I don't know how to make sense of everything that I've experienced and all that goes on in the world. But I know that I can go to God with it all and let Him know how I feel, that I'm struggling, that I don't like what's going on, that I don't agree with His response or seeming lack of action and that I want Him to do something.

Things don't always go as I think they should. There are no guarantees in life. Protection and provision don't always look like what my western way of thinking expects them to. But I have learned some powerful truths about who God is when I've relied on and trusted in Him in the most violent of storms.

He is not who I thought He was. He is something entirely different and far more incomprehensible, sovereign and powerful than I ever could have imagined. His goodness is infinitely more than I ever could have dared to dream.

I learned that there is a garden in the storm that can be accessed no other way but to go through the storm with the Lord. It is more than an undoing. It is discovering the beginning of who I am *in Him,* but only after I come to the end of my limited human comprehension and jaded worldly perspective.

Letting go of the illusion of control let me into the home of the One who is in command of everything. It's unnerving and humbling, but so worth the journey into His heart.

Letting go wasn't easy for me since I grew up in an unstable environment. It was terribly painful, exhausting and debilitating – both my childhood and letting go of control as an adult. Control was my coping skill. It made me feel safe and secure. But the Lord had other plans for me. His supernatural safety and security are wholly indescribable in earthly terms and has absolutely nothing to do with me being in "control".

Finding Him in the heart of the storm shook me to my core as only His consuming love and fear-crushing peace can do. That experience strengthened me as I came to the end of my fragile pride and frail self-reliance. I am amazed at how strong I am without hiding behind any pride, arrogance, bravado, posturing, lies, self-importance, boasting, jockeying for a position, power-dynamics and self-promotion. Once all those false helps begun to be swept out of the way, then I began to walk in confidence knowing in my heart that my identity, value and life are secure in Him. Only then did I begin to take hold of the truth that I am a daughter of the King of Heaven.

Identity is a critical thing for a warrior to own. Identity is the jugular that the devil goes for. It's what he went for in the garden by challenging Eve to consider whether God was who He said He was (trustworthy and good). It's what he went for in the wilderness during Jesus' time of testing and preparation by challenging Jesus on his identity in three separate ways.

When we take hold of the knowledge that our identity is hidden in Christ (Colossians 3:3), then we are far better prepared for and protected against the schemes of the enemy. We are also better equipped to stand against him (Ephesians 6:11), own our victories everywhere we set our foot (Joshua 1:3), step on *his* jugular (Luke 10:19) and crush *his* head underneath our feet (Romans 16:20).

Rise up all you warriors!

Acknowledgements

To the One
Who holds my heart
Who teaches me to dance on the waves
Who leads me further than I dared to dream

Thank You – for everything

A List of the Poems

Poem Title	Page
A Measure of Forgiveness	17
Arise and Fight	21
Belching Bitterness	25
Created for This	29
Forging Forgiving Strength	33
Give Them Something to Fight	37
I Know Who I Am	41
Kingdom Breathing	45
Kiss My Mockery	49
La Mujer of Light	53
Legacy of the Pharisees	57
Red Rover – I	61
Red Rover – II	65
Sticks and Stones, Too	69
the truth of Glory	73
Trusting Truth	77
Victory Light	81
Warriors from Heaven	85
Welcome to the Fray	89
you are My light	95

A Measure of Forgiveness

I cannot afford
To turn from the Lord
To let these attacks
Distract me off track

I must forgive
To be effective
To evade assault
To be light and salt

I parry and thrust
I forgive and trust
I will cut and turn
I will seek and yearn

I must navigate
Any fear and hate
And always side-step
Every sideswipe

I won't hesitate
To let hope negate
All the lies that bait
Tempt my heart to hate

Refusing to bend
Refrain to give in
Guarding heart and mind
From evil's coarse bind

Keeping clear and clean
The light within me
That burns pure and free
By Your love only

Poet's Commentary:

Unforgiveness is one of the devil's weapons that he uses to keep me from walking in freedom and peace. I cannot afford to take up this weapon, to drink this poison, to remain in the devil's prison of offense. I must stay focused on forgiveness and defend against his bait of offense.

Unforgiveness is a trap. It keeps me occupied with vengeance against my human attacker and distracted from fighting my real enemy, the devil. When I focus on the offense and the human offender, then I am disabled from attacking the devil. I am prevented from freeing the human offender from the clutches of our mutual adversary, the accuser of the brethren (see Revelation 12:10). I am essentially rendered powerless when I agree with the devil's deceptive bait to hate any human being instead of him.

The devil is my enemy. He is a gutless worm who uses human beings to carry out his evil deeds. His plans are futile. He's already lost the war. His demise is drawing nearer each day. He will pay.

The devil's war on humanity continues, for now. But the more we pursue love and mercy, the more we forgive and pray for our human enemies, then the greater dominion the Kingdom of Heaven has on this earth. When we forgive, we are partnering with the Lord to set the captives free and to release Heaven on earth.

> *He went to Nazareth, where he had been brought up, and on the Sabbath day he went into the synagogue, as was his custom. He stood up to read, and the scroll of the prophet Isaiah was handed to him. Unrolling it, he found the place where it is written:*
>
> *"The Spirit of the Lord is on me,*
>   *because he has anointed me*
>   *to proclaim good news to the poor.*
> *He has sent me to proclaim freedom*
>   *for the prisoners*
>   *and recovery of sight for the blind,*
>   *to set the oppressed free,*

*to proclaim the year of the Lord's
favor."*

*Then he rolled up the scroll, gave it back to
the attendant and sat down. The eyes of
everyone in the synagogue were fastened on
him. He began by saying to them, "Today this
scripture is fulfilled in your hearing."*
  ~ Luke 4:16-21

*your kingdom come,
your will be done,
on earth as it is in heaven,*
  ~ Matthew 6:10

Arise and Fight

To the timber on the mountain
That the Lord has called to harvest
To build a house for Himself

Let us the mighty oaks of righteousness
Come together be united
In form and structure creating
The church of the last days

A blazing city
Igniting hope
Searing through the darkness
Scorching the wicked minions
And lighting the way home
For all hearts He knows

Let us reveal the way
Remove every stumbling stone
Lead guide and uphold
All who seek His grace

Let us take up arms
Against our enemy
Defend the weak and needy
Shield the helpless and downcast
Break out those imprisoned and shackled

Let us fight
For those who cannot fight
For themselves

May we battle their enemies
as if they were our own
May we contend for their cause
As if it were our own
May we advocate for their justice
As if it were our own

May we be a voice for the oppressed
As if it were our vindication
May our hearts burn for them
As if they were our children

May our hearts burn for them
As the Father's heart burns for them
For they are all His children
Just as we are His own

Let us arise
And fight!

Poet's Commentary:

This poem is a mash up of the following Bible verses:

you also, like living stones, are being built into a spiritual house to be a holy priesthood, offering spiritual sacrifices acceptable to God through Jesus Christ.
~ 1 Peter 2:5

They will be called oaks of righteousness, a planting of the LORD for the display of his splendor
~ Isaiah 61:3

You are the light of the world. A town built on a hill cannot be hidden. Neither do people light a lamp and put it under a bowl. Instead they put it on its stand, and it gives light to everyone in the house. In the same way, let your light shine before others, that they may see your good deeds and glorify your Father in heaven.
~ Matthew 5:14-16

Defend the weak and the fatherless; uphold the cause of the poor and the oppressed.
Rescue the weak and the needy; deliver them from the hand of the wicked.
~ Psalm 82:3-4

Speak up for those who cannot speak for themselves, for the rights of all who are destitute.
Speak up and judge fairly; defend the rights of the poor and needy.
~ Proverbs 31:8-9

Belching Bitterness

Belching bitterness
To rid my insides
Of unholiness

A timely demise
Of bitterness' lies
That hindered my bliss

Expunging that mess
Led to forgiveness
Loosing all soul ties

Tenderhearted eyes
Now freed me to bless
Everyone alive

Poet's Commentary:

Bitterness is anger that has been held in for too long. It is foolish to hold on to anger, to hold it in and refuse to process it, expunge it from our souls and give it *all* over to the Lord.

> *for anger resides in the lap of fools*
> *~ Ecclesiastes 7:9*

Anger held onto for too long eats away at a person's soul and consumes their thought-life. Anger itself is not a sin, but what we do in our anger can be sinful, including holding on to our anger beyond what is healthy for us. This gives the devil access to us that he does not deserve and that he will use to wreak havoc on our souls and lives.

> *"In your anger do not sin": Do not let the sun*
> *go down while you are still angry, and do not*
> *give the devil a foothold.*
> *~ Ephesians 4:26*

It is good to process our anger and let God heal the hurt so that we can be restored in that place. We need to be released from the heavy weight of bitterness and relieved of any burden for vengeance. Nothing that we do will ever erase the wrong or make it acceptable. Vengeance increases the offense, instead of relieving or lessening it.

> *Get rid of all bitterness, rage and anger,*
> *brawling and slander, along with every form*
> *of malice. Be kind and compassionate to one*
> *another, forgiving each other, just as in Christ*
> *God forgave you.*
> *~ Ephesians 4:31-32*

Letting God restore us and forgiving our offender gives us the capacity to release the same grace and mercy to others.

Freely you have received; freely give.
~ Matthew 10:8

Forgiving others gives us victory over the devil in the area where the anger once was. Forgiveness gives us freedom from the shame and guilt associated with the event that gave rise to anger. Forgiveness gives us the ability to set more captives free, captives who live in the same prison we just walked out of.

Created for This

I was *not* created
To look for a fight

Nor was I created
To run from a fight

I was created
To conquer fear
With love

I was created
To defeat evil
With good

I was created to fiercely wield
The indestructible weapons
Of truth, mercy and love

My enemies are no match
For who I was created to be
What I was created to do
Who I was created by and for

My enemies are defeated
I was given that victory
Even before
I was ever born

I stand against the darkening
That tries to engulf me
And convince me
That I have no victory

All that I am called to fight for
Is to maintain the victory
That was already won for me
And is under my feet forever more

Poet's Commentary:

This poem, like so many other battle cries, is easy to yell when I'm safe on the sidelines and not anywhere near the real battle. It's in the times of attack that I find out whether I really am the message that I speak, whether I really believe that Jesus is my victory, whether my identity really is hidden in Christ and untouchable to my enemy.

When I wrote this poem and even when I typed it into this manuscript, I thought that I was living this message. But I was tested a few weeks later and found out that I still have areas where I fall prey to my enemy's assaults on my dignity and his lies about my identity and victory. In the moment of attack, I froze.

I know that I froze because that's what decades of brainwashing and abuse had enslaved me to do. But reminding myself of what I have to overcome and of everything I've been through didn't make the assault less horrifying or debilitating.

For weeks after the physical attack, I fought against the ensuing mental, psychological and emotional attacks. It was an intense battle for my sanity, sanctity and faith. I questioned who God was in the midst of such violence. Where was He? If He really is my shield and my protector, then how could this have happened to me? I screamed, cussed, yelled and threw things in the aftermath of the violation of my body and soul.

The thing about questioning God and expressing my anger at Him is that it means I have to acknowledge His existence and talk to Him. And talking to God is always a good place to be – no matter the content of the conversation. Talking to Him means my heart is open to Him, even if only to express my pain and anger. The Lord can do a lot with whatever little we give Him and whatever remnant is left of us after an attack. He can mend, restore and redeem *anyone* from *anything*. Even someone harmed by violence.

That's exactly what He did through our conversation over the next few weeks. He restored my defiled dignity and stained identity. He did what only He can do – give me beauty for ashes (Isaiah 61:3).

And then we went to war together! We unfroze my brain, demolished strongholds of paralyzing fear and created new neural pathways to advocacy, boldness, confidence and victory. We confronted the person who committed vile acts of violence against me. We spoke out against fear and hate. We advocated for justice, vindication and stopping this person from harming anyone else. We broke the silence and restored my voice.

My name is Rebecca, daughter of the King of kings. I *am* the message. I *am* the victory.

> *who knows but that you have come to your*
> *royal position for such a time as this?*
> *~ Esther 4:14*

Forging Forgiving Strength

Forgiveness opens the door
For me to learn more
About myself, where I'm weak
About my true enemy

With all of the harm processed
The offense released
Then I can clearly see
And adjust accordingly

When I let go of my pride
Then I am set free
To learn from my mistakes
And to improve all my ways

When I'm humble and open
Receive correction
Then able to let go
Of all that hinders my growth

Forgiveness sets me free
From the bane of bitterness
So I can learn from each event
So I can love all of me
And be released to be set free
From the burden of judging
The poison of vengeance
The illusion that either of these
Will *ever* bring me peace
Or restore what was stolen from me

Forgiveness is the key
That unlocks the prison
Drains all the poison
Trapped inside of me

Forgiveness is the path
To strengthening my soul
Forging my character
And making me all whole

Then can I walk in joy and peace
To love and accept all of me

Poet's Commentary:

Forgiveness seems so wrong to my flesh. Forgiveness seems like a denial of justice and an acquiescence to infamy. But my flesh is wrong, and the devil is a liar.

Forgiveness IS a letting go of bitterness and resentment. Forgiveness does NOT mean that the offense was not real or great. Forgiveness does NOT mean sticking my head in the sand and pretending that I wasn't attacked or harmed.

Forgiveness acknowledges the offense, the harm done and my need for comfort, healing and restoration from the Lord. Forgiveness means that I lay the offense at Jesus feet and surrender my desire for vengeance to Him. Forgiveness means that I am trusting Him to work all things for my good (Romans 8:28).

When I began to apply this new way of thinking to my life, I began to see strange and wonderful things happen. For example, when I forgave someone for cutting me off in traffic and prayed for the Lord to bless them, then almost immediately some other driver would cut off the person who had just cut me off. The Lord allowed them to reap what they sowed because I let go of my need to control the outcome, to seek vengeance, to punish my enemy for his assault on my dignity.

It is mine to avenge; I will repay.
  In due time their foot will slip;
  their day of disaster is near
    and their doom rushes upon them.
      ~ Deuteronomy 32:35

Do not gloat when your enemy falls;
  when they stumble, do not let your heart rejoice,
  or the Lord will see and disapprove
    and turn his wrath away from them.
      ~ Proverbs 24:17-18

> *Do not take revenge, my dear friends, but leave room for God's wrath, for it is written: "It is mine to avenge; I will repay," says the Lord.*
> *~ Romans 12:19*

Another example of the wonderfully strange things that happen because of my willingness to forgive: It frees my heart and mind to see and enjoy the blessings the Lord gives me. When I am focused on the offense, it blinds me to the good things in my life and sucks up all my time with obsessing about the offense and vengeance. But when I let that go by acknowledging the offense, the depth of the harm and lay it at Jesus feet, then my heart is drained of the poison of resentment, judgment and bitterness. With my heart and mind set free, I am able to acknowledge the good in each day – the victories, the relationships, the rewards and blessings. Without forgiveness there is no freedom, peace or joy.

Forgiveness also allows me to grow, to be refined and strengthened. It lets me increase in humility, patience, mercy and integrity. I am better positioned to receive God's gracious correction and merciful realignment. Forgiveness increases His likeness in me and softens my heart toward all of humanity, the ones the Lord loves. It reminds me who my real enemy is – the devil.

Forgiveness is a weapon that protects me from the schemes of the enemy. I will not take it easy on the enemy by withholding forgiveness when it is in my power to forgive an offense. Every time I forgive another human being is like kicking the devil in the teeth. Every time I pray for mercy for my human offenders I believe that I may very well be, like the martyr Steven, paving the way for the next Apostle Paul (a.k.a. Saul) to be born from the ashes of hatred (see Acts 7:57-60, 9:1-31).

I challenge you to **not** be merciful to devil. Pray for every human who harms you. Pray with a vengeance for mercy to be extended to everyone who causes you harm. Extending mercy and love to all humanity are the best offense and defense that we can use against our mutual adversary, the devil.

Give Them Something to Fight

Our fight is not with blood, bone and flesh
But we are in a fight nonetheless
And daily do we wrestle

We wrestle with God
And with ourselves
And with things not of this earth

Modern maxims claim that
We wrestle with our demons
But the truth is
They are not *our* demons
And yet
We wrestle with demons

More accurately
Demons chase us down
And torture us ad nauseum
From which we often flee
Rolling over in defeat
Beaten before even
The battle begins
Too afraid to face the fight
That rages within our mind

But we need to, we must
Stop running and turn around
To wrestle with our fear
And those little demon bitches
That torment us

Any demon's *only* authority
Is *our* authority
That we hand over to them

STOP giving them authority over *you*
They have none

STOP giving them *your* authority
That you have over them

TAKE hold of the courage
That is your birthright
TAKE your authority back
And use it to kick some demon ass

Poet's Commentary:

This poem isn't about *giving* you something to fight. It's about reminding you that we are in a battle and that it is *not* with any human being, but with the devil and his demons. It's about refocusing your anger at injustice, your frustration with the existence of evil and your desire to triumph over your enemies so that all your energy and efforts are harnessed to fight the devil and destroy his schemes for your life, my life and the lives of every other human being.

The real battle in our lives is over relationship. It's about fighting to remain focused on Jesus, fully confident in our relationship with Him – His love, truth, comfort, provision and sovereignty. The battle is about staying confident in our identity which is grounded in Him and remaining in His love and in Him who is Love.

> *For I am convinced that neither death nor life, neither angels nor demons, neither the present nor the future, nor any powers, neither height nor depth, nor anything else in all creation, will be able to separate us from the love of God that is in Christ Jesus our Lord.*
> *~ Romans 8:38-39*

With so many movies, TV shows, conferences and books about superheroes fighting against evil forces not of this world, it strikes me at how successful our enemy (the devil) is at distracting us from the real battle. The devil uses our own divine desire to defeat him against us by trivializing the battle into some fantastical idea that is outside of our grasp because of its seemingly outlandish unreality. He paints the very real supernatural war for our hearts and minds as some cartoonish thing. He tells us that only superhuman physical strength and mind control over things and human reason are the weapons that can defeat evil and win other-worldly battles.

But the devil is a liar and a perverter of the truth. We *are* in a war. The war *is* in the supernatural places (see Ephesians 6:12). And it is our *words*, our *prayers*, and our *sacrificial* love, mercy and generosity that crushes our enemy's head, causes him to tremble in fear and flee in humiliating defeat.

    This poem is about sharing with you and reminding myself just who it is that we need to fight (the devil and his unholy cohorts) and that we have supernatural strength, power and authority given to us by God to fight our other-worldly enemies. Every. Single. Day.

    Rise up and fight! This is your time! You are made for this!

I Know Who I Am

I know who I am
Beneath the scabs
I know the dormant
Me beneath the surface

I know what waits
To be remade reshaped
I know the smoldering
Fire deep within me

I know the shrinking fear
Being consumed by love
Will soon disappear
Releasing me to rise above

To step into my purpose
And take my place
Beside my King
To serve Him boldly

With honor and dignity
To reveal His mercy
His abundant love
And glory wondrous

Poet's Commentary:

Getting to know myself has been an arduous journey that only begun to get easier as I came to understand and believe that my identity truly is hidden in Christ (Colossians 3:3). Even though I am still under attack, there are parts of me that my enemy can never touch because those parts of me are safely hidden within Christ. I am learning to not fear anyone who can only harm my body but has no claim on nor ability to destroy my soul.

> *Don't be afraid of those who want to kill your*
> *body; they cannot touch your soul.*
> *~ Matthew 10:28 (NLT).*

In the midst of recovering from a recent heinous assault on my body and dignity, I am learning what Paul meant when he talked about his trials being "light and momentary troubles" and that those trials were "achieving for us an eternal glory that far outweighs them all" (2 Corinthians 4:17). The attack I survived was horrifying, but as I wrestled with God in recovery, I had an opportunity to trust Him in spite of that horrific experience. God did not cause nor did He purpose for me to have that experience, and He is more than able to restore me to wholeness no matter *what* happens to me.

I can barely put it into words what this revelation means to me, but I can say this – that it makes me feel far more powerful than I have ever felt before. I am beginning to comprehend and take hold of the knowledge that there are parts of me that are untouchable and indestructible.

Trusting God in all circumstances, especially horrific ones, brings me to a deeper understanding and depth of relationship with Him that reveals His glory even more in and through my life. I believe this is some of that "eternal glory that outweighs" my current troubles that Paul was writing about in 2nd Corinthians.

I never want to have something like that horrifying experience happen to me again, and I pray for the physical strength and help to fight off anymore such attacks, if they should come. But even if something like that should happen again, I *know* that it will not kill me nor destroy me. It will hurt me, but the Lord will restore me and redeem me. He will make me whole and ready for battle again. In fact, any such attack will *only* serve to make me stronger in faith, in spirit and in truth.

I am not as delicate as I think I am, nor as fragile as my enemy wants me to believe. I am a daughter of the King of Heaven, and my enemy has no victory over me. Ever.

Kingdom Breathing

Every second
That I am breathing
I'm making an impact
For the Kingdom

Every song I sing
Every prayer I release
Every word I speak
Is a kick in the devil's teeth

My enemy won't get a victory
Not from me
All he'll ever receive
Is defeat after defeat

Day after day
I wrestle and pray
To whoop his ass
Crush it like grass

Leaving no place
For doubt to erase
His repeated defeat
His skull under my feet

Poet's Commentary:

This poem is inspired by the warrior's psalm (Psalm 18) and this verse from the book of Romans:

> *The God of peace will soon crush Satan under your feet.*
> *~ Romans 16:20*

Sometimes I need to remind myself that everything I do advances the Kingdom, not just the books I write, the ministries I serve in, the Bible study groups I'm a part of, or anything else that is seen by others. Even the things I do in secret and the seemingly mundane things like laundry, gassing the car, grocery shopping or breathing – even those things are important to the Kingdom because I do them as a child of God and with Him in my heart and on my mind.

It's not about being successful by the world's standards or even my friends' and family's standards. It's about doing what the Lord has invited me to do, what He has called me to do. It's about serving Him even when I don't understand what it's all about or how the little that I do will make a difference.

It's about faith and trust and hope. If I could see it and understand it, then it would be easy. And it wouldn't take faith or bring Him as much glory as me trusting Him when I have no clue what He's up to and no guarantee that I will ever understand on this side of eternity.

The beauty is in the not knowing and in the trusting without seeing. It's a more fragrant offering than a million roses could ever bring Him. Seeing the joy on His face that my trust brings is a sweet reward that eclipses anything in the natural world. This is relationship. This is love. This is breathing for the Kingdom.

Kiss My Mockery

You are the God of all my days
And I am NOT afraid

The gates of hell
Can kiss my…well
You get what I mean

I will make a mockery
Of every enemy
They will beg for relief
Wishing they'd never messed with me

Poet's Commentary:

This is me mocking the devil and his unholy cohorts. I giggle a little every time I read this poem. It's simple and innocent in its content, yet wholly pure and true.

Laughing at the enemy is a quick and efficient way to disarm him. He is prideful and thrives on fear. But we, as children of God, have nothing to fear from the one who cannot destroy our souls.

It is far safer to put our fear – reverence, awe, worship and focus – in God who is trustworthy, merciful, all-powerful and sovereign over all things. This fear is a good, right, true and holy fear. It is far better to let the love of God crush all unholy fear from our hearts and minds.

> *Fear the Lord your God, serve him only and take your oaths in his name.* ~ *Deuteronomy 6:13*

> *There is no fear in love. But perfect love drives out fear, because fear has to do with punishment. The one who fears is not made perfect in love.*
> *~ 1 John 4:18*

La Mujer of Light

    You
messed with
       the wrong
   mujer

           Humanity
                  is my Padre
           Living
                  is my Madre
           Love
                  is my Vida

You have
     no
         idea
who I am
        Whose I am
               who He is

But
you're going to find out
Soon enough

Darkness must flee
from the light
blazing within me

you – will – flee
you will all flee
from His glorious light

El Senor
      es mi Dios!
Jesus
      es mi Salvador!

quien es tu dios?

Poet's Commentary:

Ever since the tower of Babel, languages have intertwined and intermingled to expand into new languages. The English spoken a thousand years ago would be foreign to me today. That old English has been influenced and nuanced by other languages (French, Italian, German – to name a few) to become the English we speak today.

Thus, it seemed fitting that I include an intermingled language poem in this collection. Growing up in a border state, I had the benefit of learning some Spanish as I grew up. I'm not perfectly fluent in the language even though I would love to do so and have prayed for the ability to become multi-lingual.

Growing up, weaving Spanish into everyday conversation was the normal for us. It's still something I embrace, enjoy and incorporate into conversations.

A good portion of the worship music I listen to is in Spanish. I understand enough of the language and the anointing on it to be moved by the Spirit. I cannot explain it except to say that when a song and worship band is anointed, I can feel it in my spirit and am moved to tears. There are things, like worship, that transcend languages and touch our hearts beyond the human words.

With the continuing transformation and influencing from other languages, who knows what any language we speak today will sound like a thousand years from now. I am certain of this though – however the language grows, it will sound beautiful and wonderful in the ears of the Lord as we worship Him in unity, spirit, truth and love.

May we never stop singing His praise in every language!

Legacy of the Pharisees

Ah! The legacy
Of the Pharisees
The strangling
Grip of rigidity
The crucifying
Lack of humility
The degrading
Whip of unmercy
The blinding
Rage of unforgiveness
The tormenting
Blight of bitterness
The deafening
Screech of unholiness
The suffocating
Gag of pridefulness
The degrading
Stench of perverseness
The enslaving
Of all that is humanity
To a lesser ruler
To merely
A created being

Poet's Commentary:

Pharisees. Teachers of the law. In today's vernacular, legalists – people who value rules for the sake of rules. People who deny that rules serve a purpose and that the purpose is greater than the rule. People who would enslave humanity to rules without any purpose other than to enslave. People who hate mercy and forgiveness because it robs them of their self-righteous superiority and lordship over those that they imprison in the rules they can't even keep themselves.

The Lord is no Pharisee. He has made it clear even before the new covenant that He values mercy over judgment and a repentant heart over a cold-hearted, prideful, token sacrifice of rule-following.

> *Does the Lord delight in burnt offerings and*
>   *sacrifices as much as in obeying the Lord?*
> *To obey is better than sacrifice,*
>   *and to heed is better than the fat of rams.*
>   *~ 1 Samuel 15:22*
>
> *You do not delight in sacrifice, or I would*
>   *bring it; you do not take pleasure in burnt*
>   *offerings.*
> *My sacrifice, O God, is a broken spirit;*
>   *a broken and contrite heart*
>   *you, God, will not despise.*
>   *~ Psalm 51:16-17*
>
> *For I desire mercy, not sacrifice,*
>   *and acknowledgment of God rather than*
>   *burnt offerings.*
>   *~ Hosea 6:6*

Letting go of legalism and embracing mercy is an inside job, as pretty much everything is. It's a condition of the heart that needs to be addressed. It's a matter of confessing my own sins, receiving the Lord's mercy and forgiveness so that I can then extend that same mercy to myself and others.

The legalism in my own heart was learned in my childhood. I was taught to hate myself and hold myself up to impossible standards. It was a cold, lonely, impoverish place to grow up in. It only got worse the older I got because, over-achiever that I was, I continued to improve upon and perfect my self-hatred.

I couldn't stand to look at myself in the mirror unless I had the mask of legalistic perfectionism on my face and was cloaked in the costume of arrogance and bravado. Those were the only things that I thought could hide my shame and insecurity. Except that I never called it shame and insecurity back then. It was a long brutal war to get past the vicious guards that kept me imprisoned in that place of self-rejection.

I was a Pharisee once. I was zealous for the lies of the enemy that demanded impossible and unreasonable standards. I believed that those lies were the truth and what kept me safe from rejection.

I know now that those lies *were* the rejection. Those lies were the prison that kept me from accepting myself as I am and even liking myself. But the lies have been exposed for what they are, and I am no longer a prisoner to self-loathing.

The Lord's love and mercy broke through the vile lies and shone on me with a tenderness that softened my heart to receive His kindness. I will speak of His great love for me and the miracles He has done in my heart. My story is of His glory! My story is only possible *because* of His boundless love and mercy!

Red Rover – I

Red rover red rover
Send all our worst over
Grace is more glorious
As seen in the worst of us

We'll take in your rejects
We'll take on your prospects
We'll redeem all your slaves
Teach them to walk on waves

Red rover red rover
Reign of death is over
The light of love has come
Leading us out of prison

We'll shake off all your lies
Wash the scales from our eyes
Free and clean, clothed in white
Armed and ready to fight

Red rover red rover
We're on our way over
We will plunder your lot
Leaving you with naught

Your kingdom will end
Into the abyss descend
Never again to rise
Goodbye father of lies

Poet's Commentary:

Standing in the gap for someone is never easy, especially not when we stand there for our human enemies. It's not easy to stand in the gap when they are throwing stones at us to murder us and destroy what we've built.

The martyr Stephen knew it wasn't easy, but he prayed for his enemies because he had faith in Jesus (see Acts 6:8-60). Stephen prayed for God to have mercy on the people who were murdering him in a slow, agonizing and brutal process by throwing stones at him until he breathed his last. Stephen prayed and a self-righteous, legalistic, judgmental gangster named Saul became a fierce and fiery apostle rebranded by God as Paul.

Who are the worst of us humans today? Hard to say. Anyone who sins against us? Gossips, backstabbers, liars, manipulators, thieves, predators, violators of decency, dignity and humanity? Who of us hasn't done at least one or more of those things? Who of us has never sinned or never harmed another human being (John 8:7)?

The thing about them, other human beings, attacking us, sinning against us, is that they have to come near the light in order to attack us. The light of Love that is in us reveals who they are and what they are about. Then we can know what to pray for them and how to pray for them. Then we can advocate for their freedom and their rebranding into fierce and fiery warriors for the Kingdom.

Their sin, in a manner of speaking, invites us to fight for them. It calls us to arms to defend and protect ourselves and to fight for their freedom, as well. It's a reckless gamble by the devil to reveal to us those whom he has enslaved, because then we know where to aim our prayer weapons of mass resurrection.

Where the devil attacks is where we need to stand in the gap. It's as simple as that. But it is by no means easy.

Will you do the easy thing? Will you ignore the real fight with the devil? Will you attack human beings who attack you?

Or will you resist the devil, pray for your human attackers and walk the harrowing and costly path of sacrificial love?

Red Rover – II

Red rover red rover
You may want to send over
Demons you think will scare us
Hoping to paralyze us

But your hopes are in vain
We are not easily slain
And even as martyrs we
Are setting captives free

The Kingdom is freedom
Breaking open your prison
Is just the beginning of
The endless reign of love

You think that you know us
Try to enslave and control us
With the little that you see
You don't know our whole being

You have no idea what
We are capable of

Red rover red rover
Do not send anyone over
For we will conquer them all
Every enemy will fall

Do not dare to attack us
For we are His righteousness
His glory burns within us
You won't be victorious

Red rover red rover
You're defeated roll over
Or suffer the consequences
Your giants beheaded by us

You sought to enslave
But only made us brave
Your weapons lacked authority
Only serving to reveal His glory

Red rover red rover
Your dominion is over
A new creation is here
Crushing all of your fear

The truth of His mercy and love
Far outweighs and rises above
All of your hate, fear and lies
You can no longer disguise

Red rover red rover
Get out and move over
Your time is almost over
Good riddance red rover

Poet's Commentary:

These are some of the verses that inspired this poem:

> *My command is this: Love each other as I have loved you. Greater love has no one than this: to lay down one's life for one's friends. You are my friends if you do what I command.*
> *~ John 15:12-14*

> *I have given you authority to trample on snakes and scorpions and to overcome all the power of the enemy; nothing will harm you.*
> *~ Luke 10:19*

> *And we know that in all things God works for the good of those who love him, who have been called according to his purpose.*
> *~ Romans 8:28*

> *For our struggle is not against flesh and blood, but against the rulers, against the authorities, against the powers of this dark world and against the spiritual forces of evil in the heavenly realms.*
> *~ Ephesians 6:12*

> *If God is for us, who can be against us?*
> *~ Romans 8:31*

Sticks and Stones, Too

Sticks and stones
Can only break bones
But words of hate
Will mutilate
The heart and soul
Don't you know

Words of fear
Spoken with a sneer
Are a slimy venom
Meant to taint and poison
Everyone who hears
Those violent jeers

Verbal violence
Rips through and rends
Destroys and rejects
Relational covenant
Violating what the heart wants
Honest acceptance

The truth of those who speak
From hate and fear reveal
They hate themselves
Even more than everyone else
They try to purge with every word
Hurt that can only be healed by the Lord

Sticks and stones
Sighs and groans
Let our voices
Reveal our choices
To stand in the gap
When we are attacked

Poet's Commentary:

Words are not empty and powerless even if we treat them that way. Words have weight. They have authority. They can harm the soul, or they can strengthen and encourage the soul.

> *The tongue has the power of life and death,*
> *and those who love it will eat its fruit.*
> *~ Proverbs 18:21*

It is foolishness to deny the value of words when everyone of us carries scars unseen buried deep within our souls of verbal assaults on our dignity. Only facing this debilitating weapon and disarming the enemy of it will bring us the healing and peace that we crave and desperately need.

Here are a few of my weapons – prayers of scriptural truth – that I use when attacked with curses:

> *Like a fluttering sparrow or a darting swallow,*
> *an undeserved curse does not come to rest.*
> *~ Proverbs 26:2*

And Numbers 23 – Here's a synopsis: Balak attempts to hire Balaam to curse the Israelites as they wander in the desert. Balaam warns Balak that he can only speak what the Lord tells him. Balaam then proceeds to speak the words the Lord gives him. Three times Balaam blesses the Israelites, and four times he curses the Israelites' enemies.

From this passage of scripture, I learned that even if my enemies want to curse me, the Lord can turn the curses of my enemies into blessings.

the truth of Glory

If I sugarcoat my story
Then I diminish His glory
Don't ask me to tell you
Anything less than truth

I won't sanitize
The reality of my story
So you can remain in lies
That deny His sovereignty

I won't minimize
The beauty of His mercy
Revealed through my life
In my story of His glory

He has rescued me from my enemy
He has washed me clean of infamy
He has healed my fractured soul
He has remade my heart whole

I will *never* stop singing
Of His goodness and mercy
I will *never* stop rejoicing
In His love poured out over me

Your fear cannot silence me
His love now has set me free
I am always in His heart
From there I will *not* depart

Poet's Commentary:

If I don't tell you where I was, what's been done to me and what I've done, then I'm *not* revealing the fullness of God's grace and mercy in my life. Without the truth of the fall, the cross is pointless and too cruel to comprehend.

If you're not ready to hear the truth or scared that talking about sin will multiply it, then don't come near me because I can't stop telling of His glory and of all that He's done for me. And don't read these verses because they testify to the power of testimony:

> *Let the redeemed of the Lord tell their story –*
> *those he redeemed from the hand of the foe.*
> *~ Psalm 107:2*

> *They triumphed over him by the blood of the*
> *Lamb and by the word of their testimony.*
> *~ Revelation 12:11*

Trusting Truth

Truth covers shame
Better than a fig leaf
Better than anything

Though lies expose
Uncovering to shame
And maligning to fear

Yet truth reveals
And exposes the lies
Thus realigning to love

Truth speak
Brings sweet release
Liberates the soul
Unlocks the whole
Unties that bind
Restores the mind
Gushes in relief
Joy unleashed

Freedom abounds
When truth expounds
Limitless endless
Boundless shameless
Beautiful
Loving truth

Poet's Commentary:

Adam and Eve tried to hide their shame and nakedness with leaves. But only the truth would have covered their nakedness and set them free from any shame. Truth also would have honored their relationship with God.

> *When the woman saw that the fruit of the tree was good for food and pleasing to the eye, and also desirable for gaining wisdom, she took some and ate it. She also gave some to her husband, who was with her, and he ate it. Then the eyes of both of them were opened, and they realized they were naked; so, they sewed fig leaves together and made coverings for themselves.*
> *~ Genesis 3:6-7*

The Apostle Paul had some insight into the value the Lord places on truth and its importance in relationship. In Ephesians, Paul talks about putting on spiritual armor. He lists out the pieces of armor that a Roman soldier wore in those days.

> *Therefore put on the full armor of God, so that when the day of evil comes, you may be able to stand your ground, and after you have done everything, to stand. Stand firm then, with the belt of truth buckled around your waist, with the breastplate of righteousness in place, and with your feet fitted with the readiness that comes from the gospel of peace. In addition to all this, take up the shield of faith, with which you can extinguish all the flaming arrows of the evil one. Take the helmet of salvation and the sword of the Spirit, which is the word of God.*
> *~ Ephesians 6:13-17*

What I used to miss in understanding this passage had to do

with the belt of truth, until I did some research on what the belt portion of a Roman soldier's armor looked like. A belt was *not* an accessory, like it is today. And Roman soldiers didn't wear pants, so the belt's purpose was not to hold up their pants.

Roman soldiers wore a tunic, kind of like a knee length shirtdress, underneath their armor. On top of the tunic, they placed the breastplate which protected their chest and the belt which protected something else. As it turns out, the belt protected them from the waist to the knees and was actually more like a skirt or a kilt – a seriously heavy-duty kilt.

The belt was made up of a large heavy leather strap that went around the soldier's waist, like a modern-day belt, but it also served as a waistband for the other parts that made up the belt/kilt. Attached along the entire length of this waistband were thick heavy straps of leather, about 5 inches wide, that hanged down and extended from the waistband to the knees with the bottom of each strap weighed down by a heavy piece of metal. The weight at the bottom of the straps kept the "kilt" in place and from blowing up on a windy day or in the midst of battle. In addition to all this leather that made up the "kilt", the area right in front of the genitals was also covered by smaller yet weighty straps of metal, as a special covering for this sensitive area. This provided extra protection for the most vulnerable parts of the body.

From this understanding of a Roman soldiers' armor, it's clear that the belt covers a significant and vital portion of a soldier's body. This is the belt of truth Paul teaches about, and it covers the same area that Adam and Eve tried to hide from God once they ate the fruit of the tree of the knowledge of good and evil.

I know in my own life it's not easy to own the truth when I've sinned or made a mistake that hurts relationship. But I do know that every time that I take the risk and choose truth, humility and vulnerability, that decision leads to freedom and hope for restoration of the relationship. Truth that springs forth from love honors God, relationship, others and myself. It preserves and protects dignity.

> *Then you will know the truth, and the truth*
> *will set you free.*
> *~ John 8:32*

Being truthful covers my shame better than anything else ever could.

Victory Light

Darkness engulfed me
Attempting to infect me
To murder me
With its poisonous hatred

But the Light
Was all around me
Pursuing my soul
Relentlessly

Covering me where
And when it could
Without violating my will
Or sanctity

Diligent, vigilant
The Light
Never left my side

Vengeant, protective
Love's light
Always shone in my life

It broke through
The barriers of fear and abuse
To rescue
My broken soul torn through

This fiercest of loves
Never gave up
Though I pushed it away
Every single day

Until my soul saw
That this love is faithful
Beyond reason and doubt

Until I knew
In my head and heart
That He is

Who He Says He Is

Poet's Commentary:

Knowing God is more than a one-time event. It's a process of ever-increasing discovery, adventure and exploration into the One who is infinite. Even more than that, it's His process of pursuing me, earning my trust, winning me over, tenderizing my heart, revealing Himself to me little by little as I am able to receive truth from Him.

Knowing Him is more about *Him* revealing Himself to me than it is about *me* discovering Him. It's all His choice, His victory. I wouldn't have chosen Him if He hadn't first chosen me. I wouldn't love Him if He hadn't pursued me when I was His enemy and convinced me that He is trustworthy. I wouldn't know His love if He hadn't given it to me freely and waited patiently for me to accept Him.

I've done nothing to deserve His love and friendship. But He gives it to me anyway without restriction or restraint, without any strings attached, without a trick up His sleeve. He just gives love – freely, generously, lavishly, abundantly.

He is love. It sounds so simple, yet to experience even a little of His love is crushing and terrifying in a holy and exhilarating way. If He didn't love me, I wouldn't be here writing this book right now. I wouldn't be free of my past. I wouldn't be the woman I've become. I would not ever have known love. I am because He is. His light and love are the victory over my life.

Warriors from Heaven

When the sweetness of intimacy
Is given up for bullying speed
And ram-rodding violent action
Then haste makes waste of what was good

It kills the beauty
To ensnare
With only a promise
Of the beauty that
Once was there

It gives merely
An illusion
To entice purely
With delusion
The minds wobbly
From the intrusion

Weakened defenses
Fall swiftly
To these offenses
That deftly
Blast through fences

Left lonely
Abandoned hence
To suffer
Cruel violence

Will no one
Come to their defense?
Are none left
That are heaven sent?
Who will lift
Hands to rend the heavens
And call forth
Righteous redemption?

Arise and fight
Warriors from heaven!

Poet's Commentary:

As children of God, we are called to be priests, to pray for those who need salvation and mercy. It is our honor to stand in the gap for those who have yet to be set free from the prison of our enemy.

> *I have posted watchmen on your walls, Jerusalem;*
> *they will never be silent day or night.*
> *You who call on the Lord,*
> *give yourselves no rest,*
> *and give him no rest till he establishes Jerusalem*
> *and makes her the praise of the earth.*
> *~ Isaiah 62:6-7*

Constant intercession is what Jesus, our great high priest, did for us and continues to do for us (see Romans 8:34). He knows what it is to be human and weak. He intercedes for us accordingly (see Hebrews 4:14-16). The Lord has great mercy and compassion on us even before we know Him or love Him. He invites us to do the same for others – to pray for them even if they are against us, to passionately intercede for them and to advocate for their freedom.

> *You have not gone up to the breaches in the wall to repair it for the people of Israel so that it will stand firm in the battle on the day of the Lord.*
> *~ Ezekiel 13:5*

The Lord is looking and waiting for us to step into the gaps in the defenses and pray for the wounded and weary, for those who don't know how to pray, for those who can't speak for themselves.

> *Speak up for those who cannot speak for themselves,*
> *for the rights of all who are destitute.*
> *~ Proverbs 31:8*

Welcome to the Fray

You're under attack
There's a fight
Get off your ass
Get your armor on
And fight back
This is your time
It's your turn to attack
This is your fight
This is no time to be slack

Welcome to the fray
Kicking demon ass every day

Don't worry that you'll miss
The fight coming for you
They won't let go of
The foothold assault on you
It's really just a matter of
How you choose to
Respond to their villainy
Will you passively submit
Handing over your authority
Like a whipped bitch
Or rise up and fight to sustain
The victory *He* already obtained

You are no one's prey
You are no one's filthy fool
You are strong in faith
You need to know truth
You can do anything
Because God is with you

Will you choose to
Fight in the fray?

Or will you let them
Take your life away?

The choice is yours –
Choose to fight!
Choose your life!

Poet's Commentary:

The devil is attacking us. We don't get to choose whether or not we will be attacked. However, we do get to choose how we will respond to these assaults on our dignity, humanity and faith. Don't stick your head in the sand thinking that your self-imposed ignorance will keep you safe from the attacks. Doing so will only make you more vulnerable to attack, easier prey for your enemy and living less than in the fullness of victory. Remember that Moses *only* qualification for his calling was that God would be with him.

> *But Moses said to God, "Who am I that I should go to Pharaoh and bring the Israelites out of Egypt?"*
>
> *And God said, "I will be with you.*
> *~ Exodus 3:11-12*

Remember that the Lord repeatedly told Joshua, Moses' protégé and successor, to be courageous and that the Lord would give him victory everywhere he set his foot.

> *Have I not commanded you? Be strong and courageous. Do not be afraid; do not be discouraged, for the Lord your God will be with you wherever you go.*
> *~ Joshua 1:9*

Even though I talk about "kicking demon ass" in this poem, the focus isn't the devil and his maniacal minions. My intent with this line is to point us back to the where the real fight lies – the supernatural realm.

> *For our struggle is not against flesh and blood, but against the rulers, against the authorities, against the powers of this dark world and against the spiritual forces of evil in the heavenly realms.*
> *~ Ephesians 6:12*

The true focus is the victory we have in Jesus and defending against the attacks that our enemy launches at us in an attempt to dislodge us from our godly stronghold that is Jesus Christ, our Lord and Savior. Everything we need is found in Him. But that doesn't mean that the battle is easy or that it will go as we think it should or want it to.

The first century church knew who God was in the midst of horrific persecution – crucifixions, beheadings, burned alive as human torches, upside down crucifixions, and so on. Even today, there are parts of the world in which Christians face ghastly physical persecution and life-and-death decisions regarding their faith.

We know little of this type of battle in the western world except what we see reported in the media. The attacks we are under are more subtle, but they are no less deadly in their intent to defile our identity, dismantle our dignity and destroy our faith.

We need to wake up to the reality of this war and respond as warriors should – on our knees in violent wrestling prayer that rends the heavens and shakes our demon attackers to their core!

All of us believers are collectively the Body of Christ. Let us stand in unity against an enemy who seeks to destroy us all.

Our faith wasn't birthed in comfort and ease, luxury and wealth, peace and freedom. It was born in poverty and struggle, lack and challenge, conflict and prison. It was baptized in fire and spirit. It is not for the faint of heart to be Christian. There will be battles. There will be trials and tests. There will be difficult decisions that have no easy answer and no guaranteed outcome in this life. Sometimes the promises are carried through in later generations and times even though we are the ones planting the seeds of faith in those promises (John 4:38 and Hebrews 11:13-16).

This is what it means to walk by faith not by sight, to not know how we're going to get to where we're going, only knowing that the Lord is with us each step of the way. The path is narrow and steep. It is often lonely and barren. But it births us over and over again into an increasingly glorious creation, a reflection of the glory of the Lord who lives and makes His home within us.

Welcome to the fray. Welcome to the Way. Welcome to the unity of the Bride of Christ.

This day I call the heavens and the earth as witnesses against you that I have set before

you life and death, blessings and curses. Now choose life, so that you and your children may live and that you may love the Lord your God, listen to his voice, and hold fast to him. For the Lord is your life, and he will give you many years in the land he swore to give to your fathers, Abraham, Isaac and Jacob.
~ Deuteronomy 30:19-20

For God so loved the world that he gave his one and only Son, that whoever believes in him shall not perish but have eternal life.
~ John 3:16

Choose life!
Choose Jesus Christ!

you are My light

In the midst of this place
you reveal My face

In this frenzied city
you give them a glimpse of Me

Against the chaos and noise
you release Peace through your voice

You bring the calming center
to every place you enter

Your spirit of gentleness
awakens the same in them

Love's refreshing breeze
washes over them gently
flowing from your face
releasing My grace

From within you My light
shines forth warm and bright
no one can hide nor deny
the beauty *I Am* in your eyes

Poet's Commentary:

This poem is what I believe the Lord speaks over me. He loves me and created me to be a reflection of Who He Is so that I can reveal Him to those around me. He placed something of Himself in me that can only be seen and known by seeing and knowing me.

I believe the same is true for each human being that He has and will ever create. The more we see and know each other, the more we see and know of Him.

As we reveal Who He Is, we release His Kingdom on earth. As we partner with Him and allow Him to continue to refine us and reshape us into His image, we reveal ever more of Him and His love for all humanity. We are His representatives and messengers of grace, mercy, love and peace.

> *You are the light of the world. A town built on a hill cannot be hidden. Neither do people light a lamp and put it under a bowl. Instead they put it on its stand, and it gives light to everyone in the house. In the same way, let your light shine before others, that they may see your good deeds and glorify your Father in heaven.*
> *~ Matthew 5:14-16*

> *And we all, who with unveiled faces contemplate the Lord's glory, are being transformed into his image with ever-increasing glory, which comes from the Lord, who is the Spirit.*
> *~ 2 Corinthians 3:18*

> *For we are God's handiwork, created in Christ Jesus to do good works, which God prepared in advance for us to do.*
> *~ Ephesians 2:10*

*Let the redeemed of the Lord tell their story
those he redeemed from the hand of the foe
~ Psalm 107:2*

About the Author

Rebecca Anne Perry has a soft voice, a bold spirit and a self-proclaimed knock-down-drag-out kind of faith. She survived tremendous childhood trauma and now walks out each day on an intentional path of increasing freedom. Because of the abuse she endured, she connected to her creativity much later in life and is on a journey of exploring, accepting and learning to enjoy being creative.

She is a quiet influencer who is discovering how to live an authentic and sincere life, making more mistakes in the process than she wants to admit, and learning to accept and delight in her humanity a little more each day.

You can discover more books by Rebecca, listen to some of her poetry readings, learn about her journey and find out about her upcoming projects on her website:

www.RebeccaAnnePerry.com